Contents

W9-CCJ-769

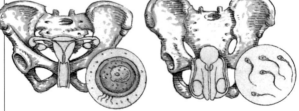

CAUTION!! It's fine to get help from your parents if you need it, but don't let them put the skeleton together by themselves! Adults rarely read or follow directions. See the guide on pages 7–9.

You and Your Bones

Imagine yourself with no bones at all—no backbone or leg bones to hold you up, no skull or ribs to cover your soft insides. You'd be a big, pulsating blob, stuck in the same spot for the rest of your life!

The bones of your skeleton give you shape and support. They keep your brain, heart, lungs, and other fragile organs from getting bounced around and bruised. And they team up with your muscles to help you move.

Just to take one small step forward, about 200 muscles are needed to move your leg bones, shift your balance, and steady your body so you won't fall over. And they're not working alone. Blood cells are busy delivering food and oxygen for energy, and the brain is transmitting detailed directions on when and how to move. Whether you're

X-rays can "see" through your skin to the bones inside; otherwise, your skeleton is invisible!

sitting still or running at full speed, every part of your body has a specific assignment —and all the parts must work together to keep you alive and well.

Every time you stand up or sit down, chew your food, or even listen to your favorite music, your bones are on the job— without any direct orders from you!

This book will introduce you to your own skeleton and explain how it works with the rest of your body. You'll discover how you react to the outside world, how you move, and how you think. You'll find projects to do, either on your own or with a "skeleton crew" of friends, as well as Body Watch boxes that describe your body's built-in safety measures. You'll learn what happens to food after it's chewed and swallowed, how you "shrink" during the day and "grow" again at night, and why you yawn, hiccup, and get goose bumps.

This is a guide to your body—make no bones about it!

Life Without Bones

The first forms of animal life, almost 600 million years ago, had no backbones in their small, simple bodies. Today their backbone-less descendants, called invertebrates, include insects and worms, starfish and jellyfish—members of a group that comprises over 97% of the animals on our planet. Insects alone outnumber human beings by a staggering ratio of 200 million to one!

Boning Up

The bones that come with this book fit together to form an accurate model of an adult human skeleton. Just pop the bones into place, and move them individually to see how your own skeleton works.

When not in use, the model can stay on display in its own see-through case.

1 *Front of skull*
2 *Upper rear skull*
3 *Lower rear skull*
4 *Jaw*
5 *Right shoulder blade*
6 *Left shoulder blade*
7 *Collarbone*
8 *Spine*
9 *Upper left arm*
10 *Upper right arm*
11 *Lower right arm*
12 *Lower left arm*
13 *Stand clip*
14 *Stand*
15 *Right hand*
16 *Left hand*
17 *Right rib cage*
18 *Left rib cage*
19 *Right pelvis*
20 *Left pelvis*
21 *Upper right leg*
22 *Upper left leg*
23 *Lower right leg*
24 *Lower left leg*
25 *Right foot*
26 *Left foot*

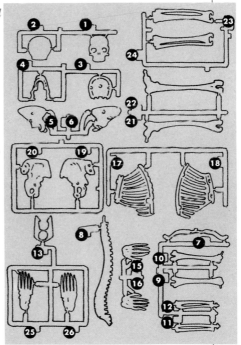

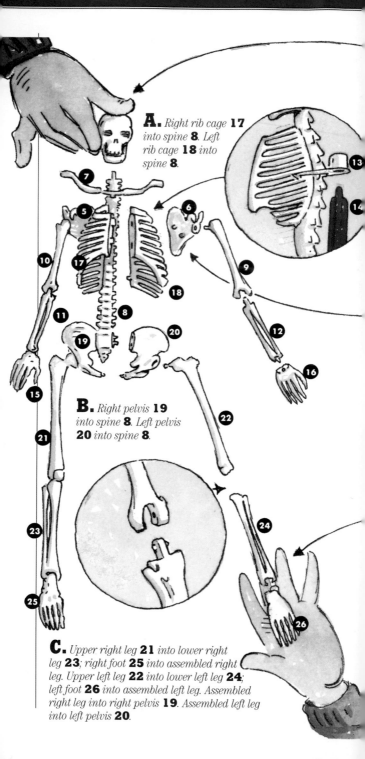

A. *Right rib cage* **17** *into spine* **8.** *Left rib cage* **18** *into spine* **8.**

B. *Right pelvis* **19** *into spine* **8.** *Left pelvis* **20** *into spine* **8.**

C. *Upper right leg* **21** *into lower right leg* **23;** *right foot* **25** *into assembled right leg. Upper left leg* **22** *into lower left leg* **24;** *left foot* **26** *into assembled left leg. Assembled right leg into right pelvis* **19.** *Assembled left leg into left pelvis* **20.**

D. *Lower rear skull* **3** *into upper rear skull* **2**. *Front of skull* **1** *into assembled rear skull. Jaw* **4** *into assembled skull. Assembled skull into spine* **8**.

E. *Right shoulder blade* **5** *into right rib cage* **17**. *Left shoulder blade* **6** *into left rib cage* **18**. *Collarbone* **7** *into rib cage* **17** *and* **18**. *Upper right arm* **10** *into lower right arm* **11**; *right hand* **15** *into assembled right arm. Upper left arm* **9** *into lower left arm* **12**; *left hand* **16** *into assembled left arm. Assembled left arm into left shoulder blade* **6**. *Assembled right arm into right shoulder blade* **5**. *Stand clip* **13** *into rib cage* **17** *and* **18**. *Stand* **14** *into clip* **13**.

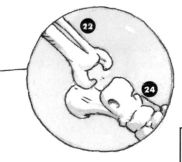

Make sure you know your left foot from your right! When the skeleton is facing you, its left side will appear to be on the right—and vice versa.

Bone Directory

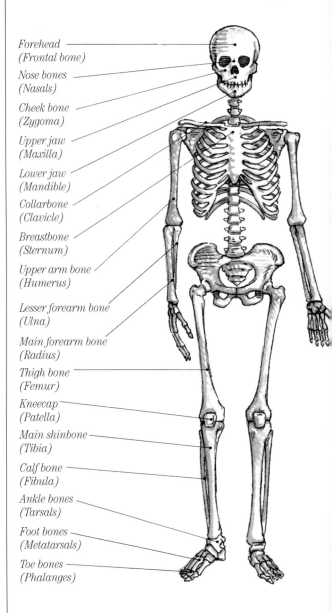

Forehead
(Frontal bone)

Nose bones
(Nasals)

Cheek bone
(Zygoma)

Upper jaw
(Maxilla)

Lower jaw
(Mandible)

Collarbone
(Clavicle)

Breastbone
(Sternum)

Upper arm bone
(Humerus)

Lesser forearm bone
(Ulna)

Main forearm bone
(Radius)

Thigh bone
(Femur)

Kneecap
(Patella)

Main shinbone
(Tibia)

Calf bone
(Fibula)

Ankle bones
(Tarsals)

Foot bones
(Metatarsals)

Toe bones
(Phalanges)

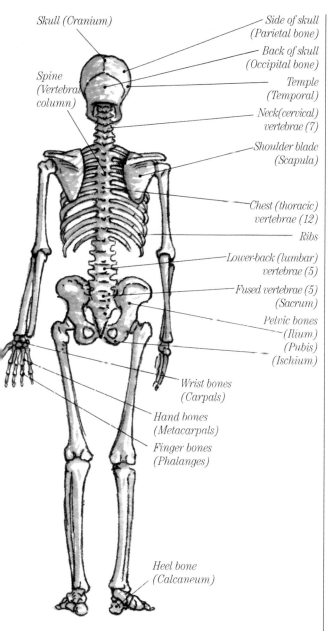

Skull (Cranium)

Side of skull (Parietal bone)

Back of skull (Occipital bone)

Spine (Vertebral column)

Temple (Temporal)

Neck (cervical) vertebrae (7)

Shoulder blade (Scapula)

Chest (thoracic) vertebrae (12)

Ribs

Lower-back (lumbar) vertebrae (5)

Fused vertebrae (5) (Sacrum)

Pelvic bones (Ilium) (Pubis) (Ischium)

Wrist bones (Carpals)

Hand bones (Metacarpals)

Finger bones (Phalanges)

Heel bone (Calcaneum)

Many bones have two names: a common name, and a scientific name derived from Latin or Greek words describing their appearance, function, or location. The three small bones in the ear, for example, are named for their shape: the hammer (malleus), the anvil (incus), and the stirrup (stapes).

Bone Basics

You may not realize it, but your bones are alive and growing inside you. Tiny bone-building cells are constantly at work, shaping your skeleton from one day to the next. First come the osteoblasts, which cruise along the bones' growth surfaces and build layers of a protein material called collagen. Then particles of the mineral calcium phosphate get stuck in the collagen and crystallize to form new bone.

Much of this growth is taking place in the gap between the shaft and the end of each bone. By the time your skeleton reaches

Fifty percent of a bone's weight comes from minerals. A third of each bone is protein, and the rest is mostly water.

Most growth in the long bones of the arms and legs occurs in the cartilage that separates the end from the shaft.

Blood vessels

Spongy bone

The longest bone in your body, and perhaps the strongest, is the thigh bone (pictured here). Its long shaft is a tube with outside walls of very thick, solid bone to withstand all the bending, twisting, and impact forces caused by your active life.

adult size, around age 20 or so, all the tough, milk-colored cartilage that fills the gap will have turned to bone.

While your bones are growing, your skeleton not only gets bigger but also changes its proportions. When you were only a few days old, for example, your head was as big around as your chest and about a quarter the length of your body. When you reach adulthood, your head will be half as big around as your chest and only about one-seventh of your body length!

Small pores, or holes, leading from the outside into the interior, allow blood vessels through to nourish the bone and carry away wastes.

Marrow

Dense outer layer of compact bone

Vanishing Bones

In your lifetime, you'll "lose" about 600 bones! Before you were born, your skeleton contained over 800 separate bones, many of which grew or fused together so that you had about 450 at birth. By age 20, when your bones have finished growing and the separate parts have joined together, they'll number only about 206.

Curious Cartilage

Long before you were born, your skeleton was made completely of cartilage—the same rubbery substance you see at the fat end of a chicken "drumstick." Gradually, the temporary cartilage hardened and became bone. Some cartilage, however, such as the wiggly end of your nose and the outer part of your ear, is permanent and will never harden into bone. This type is also found in the disks between the vertebrae of your spine and at the ends of bones where they meet a joint.

In old age, the disk cartilage shrinks, but some permanent cartilage grows larger—and may cause your ears and nose to grow!

The Wonder of Bones

How can bones be strong enough to carry your weight, yet light enough not to slow you down? Bones get their amazing strength from calcium, phosphorus, and other minerals—some of the same minerals found in rocks. And your skeleton doesn't feel heavy because all the long bones are hollow!

Still, this doesn't mean that bones are empty. In the otherwise hollow interior of many bones is a substance called marrow, which manufactures most of your blood cells. Without these cells, the rest of the cells in your body would wither and die.

Cells:

The Body's Building Blocks

Visible only through a microscope, cells are the smallest units of the living tissues that make up your body structure. Different types of cells, each with separate assignments, form specific kinds of tissue. Bone cells clump together to make bone tissue; muscle cells, whose

Nerve cell

function is to move the bones, create the muscle tissue that actually does the job.

Muscle cells

Cells are always dividing in two to make more cells. Some new cells add to your overall growth, while others serve as replacements for the three billion cells that die every minute. Body cells also get bigger. When you reach adulthood, your heart will be 16 times larger than when you first came into the world.

Red blood cell

Just think—your life begins as a single cell, the fertilized egg in your mother's body, and in just about 40 weeks you grow to become a human being!

White blood cell

Muscle Power

Without the muscles attached to your skeleton, you'd be stuck in one place like a useless "bag of bones"— doing nothing and going nowhere!

Muscles work extremely hard. Around your eyes are little muscles that contract 100,000 times a day!

Every single part of your body has muscles, working nonstop to keep you lively and on the go.

Some 650 muscles cover your skeleton to hold your bones in place and make them move. Attached at both ends by tough cords of tissue called tendons, these skeletal muscles work in pairs to pull the bones into position. You can observe your muscles at work by placing your left hand on the large biceps muscle of your upper right arm as you bend the arm into a "strongman" pose. The

The long, thin fibers of skeletal, or voluntary, muscles are laid out in rows side by side and contract more rapidly than other muscle fibers.

Muscle Sense

Electrical signals from the muscles let your brain know your position at all times. Thanks to this "muscle sense," you can cross a room without looking down to make sure that one foot is properly placed in front of the other.

muscle will bulge as it shortens, or contracts, to pull up your forearm. Under your right arm is the relaxed triceps muscle. Straighten your arm, and feel the biceps relax, or lengthen, as the triceps tightens to pull your forearm down.

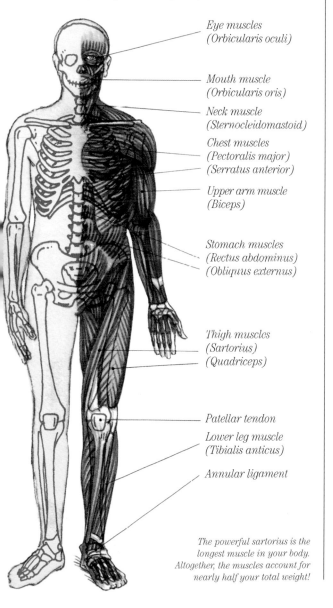

Eye muscles
(Orbicularis oculi)

Mouth muscle
(Orbicularis oris)

Neck muscle
(Sternocleidomastoid)

Chest muscles
(Pectoralis major)
(Serratus anterior)

Upper arm muscle
(Biceps)

Stomach muscles
(Rectus abdominus)
(Obliquus externus)

Thigh muscles
(Sartorius)
(Quadriceps)

Patellar tendon

Lower leg muscle
(Tibialis anticus)

Annular ligament

The powerful sartorius is the longest muscle in your body. Altogether, the muscles account for nearly half your total weight!

Contractions of skeletal muscles are started by electrical signals from the brain, and the strength of each contraction depends on the number of signals. For example, you use the same muscles whether you pick up a brick or a pencil, but when you pick up the brick there might be 50 times as many signals!

Independent Muscles

Skeletal muscles work *voluntarily* which means they follow commands from your brain, but other muscles are beyond your conscious control. These smooth, *involuntary* muscles line the internal

*Upper back muscle
(Trapezius)*

*Shoulder muscle
(Deltoid)*

*Upper arm muscle
(Triceps)*

*Back muscles
(Infraspinatus)
(Latissimus dorsi)*

*Buttock muscles
(Gluteus medius)
(Gluteus maximus)*

*Hamstring muscles
(Biceps femoris)
(Semitendinosus)
(Semimembranosus)*

*Calf muscle
(Gastrocnemius)*

Achilles tendon

With all our human strength, we can never match the real musclemen of the animal world. Most insects can lift 20 times their own weight!

organs such as the stomach, blood vessels, and lungs. Operating on their own, day and night, involuntary muscles push food through your digestive tract, keep your blood circulating, and enable you to breathe—all without any thought on your part.

The heart muscle has a different structure, but luckily you don't have to remember to make it beat, either!

The fibers of smooth, or involuntary, muscles cross over each other to allow stretching or contracting in two different directions.

Powerful cardiac muscle fibers form the wall of the heart. These small, often branched, fibers attach end to end.

Feel It In Your Bones

To demonstrate the benefit of using your muscles as levers, try lifting a brick two different ways. First, hold your arm out straight, grip the brick from the top, and raise it in the air without bending your elbow. Difficult, isn't it?

Using the bones as levers, opposite muscle pairs such as the biceps and triceps alternately contract and relax to bend or straighten the arm.

Now, without changing your grip, turn the brick over so that it rests in your palm and pull it up toward your shoulder as you bend your arm. This way is easier because your muscles worked on the "lever principle," pulling against the bone.

Pickup and Delivery:

The Circulatory System at Work

Fresh from the bone marrow, new red and white blood cells pass into the bloodstream and begin their journey through the 60,000-mile (96,500-kilometer) network known as the circulatory system.

Floating in a pale fluid called plasma, the red cells pick up oxygen from the lungs and little bits of food from the digestive tract and deliver them as fuel for the rest of the body's cells. The far less numerous white cells patrol the bloodstream to fight infection by attacking germs.

Feel It In Your Bones

Measure your own heartbeat by placing your fingertips on the pulse at the inside of your wrist, about three finger-widths from the base of the thumb toward the elbow. (Be sure not to use your thumb, which has a pulse of its own.) You'll feel blood being pumped through your wrist on its way to your hand at a rate of approximately 72 to 75 beats per minute when your body is at rest. Women have slightly higher heart rates than men. Athletes of both sexes can have much lower resting heart rates—down to about 50 beats per minute!—because exercise has trained their hearts to deliver a higher volume of blood with each beat.

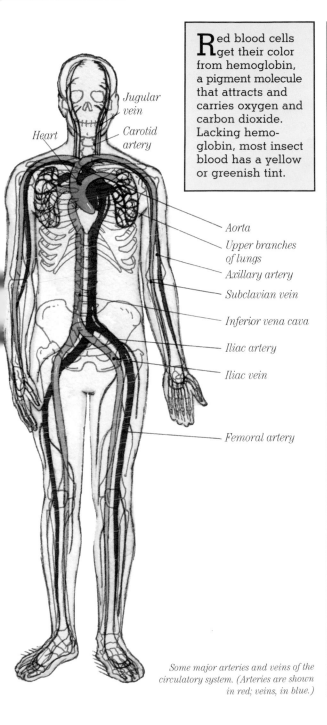

R ed blood cells get their color from hemoglobin, a pigment molecule that attracts and carries oxygen and carbon dioxide. Lacking hemoglobin, most insect blood has a yellow or greenish tint.

Jugular vein

Carotid artery

Heart

Aorta

Upper branches of lungs

Axillary artery

Subclavian vein

Inferior vena cava

Iliac artery

Iliac vein

Femoral artery

Some major arteries and veins of the circulatory system. (Arteries are shown in red; veins, in blue.)

The power center of the circulatory system is the heart, beating day and night inside the rib cage to pump blood through the arteries, veins, and capillaries. A little larger than your fist, the heart receives blood from the veins and sends it to the lungs for oxygen. Bright red, oxygenated blood returns to the heart and is pumped out through smaller and smaller arteries until it enters the capillaries, whose thin walls permit food bits and oxygen to pass right through to the body cells.

Blood cells line up single file to pass through the narrowest capillaries.

Meanwhile, in the opposite direction, wastes squeeze into the bloodstream through the capillary walls to be carried in veins to the organs that dispose of them. Carbon dioxide, for example, is taken to the lungs and expelled from your body every time you breathe out; other wastes are processed in the kidneys and liver.

It seems like a long journey, with many tasks along the way, but one round trip through the circulatory system takes only about 60 seconds—and the cells make the trip about 1,400 times a day!

To the Rescue!

When you cut your finger or scrape your knee, white cells in the vicinity move in and "chew up" any invading germs. Broken bits of blood cells called platelets,

Your body's repair team races to the site of a cut. Platelets clump together to form a plug, while white blood cells cruise the bloodstream to attack bacteria and other invaders.

originating in bone marrow, also go to work at the emergency site by clumping together to seal off the broken blood vessels. Clotting, or coagulation, takes place when chemicals from the platelets combine with other substances in the blood and form a scab over the cut or scrape.

The Heart of the Matter

Pulmonary veins

Left atrium (receives blood from the lungs via the pulmonary veins)

Valve separating atrium from ventricle

Right atrium (receives blood from the body through the superior and inferior vena cava)

Heart muscle

Two pumps in the heart work side by side to keep blood circulating. The right-hand pump forces oxygen-spent blood to the lungs, while the left-hand pump squeezes oxygen-rich blood out to the rest of the body through the arteries.

Each pump has two chambers: an atrium and a ventricle. As blood travels from one to the other, small valves open and shut to keep it on course. What you hear when you listen to your heartbeat is the sound of these valves slamming shut.

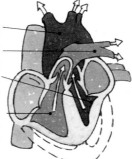

Aorta

Pulmonary artery

Left ventricle (pushes blood out to the body's tissues through the aorta)

Right ventricle (pushes blood out to the lungs through the pulmonary artery)

The heart is made of the strongest muscle in your body. In one year, it beats almost 40 million times.

The Skull and Sensory Organs

The human skull appears to be one large, rounded bone with a separate piece for the lower jaw, but in reality it consists of 29 different bones! Fifteen are found in the jigsaw puzzle of the face, where sockets protect the eyes, nose bones guard air openings, and upper and lower jaw bones encase the tongue and teeth. Six small bones deep within the skull are used in hearing. And the eight thick bones that form the cranium, the major part of the skull behind the face, safeguard the brain from hard knocks.

Babies are born with gaps between their skull bones, leaving soft spots covered by skin. For the first few months,

— Frontal bone (forehead)

— Parietal bone

— Temporal bone

— Nasal bone

— Zygoma (cheekbone)

— Maxilla (upper jaw)

— Mandible (lower jaw)

Your "solid" skull is made up of many parts—28 plus the lower jaw.

Semicircular
canals

Malleus
(hammer)

Incus
(anvil)

Stapes
(stirrup)

Eustachian tube

*Deep inside your skull, at the end
of the ear canals, are the six
smallest bones in your body.
Vibrations set up in these bones
allow you to hear!*

before the bones grow together,
you can see the largest soft spot beating at
the top of a baby's head as blood is pumped
to the brain!

Not Just for Chewing

Rooted in the spongy bone of your jaws, your
teeth are used for biting and grinding food,
giving shape to your face, and making certain
speech sounds. The first teeth to come in are the
"baby teeth" (or "milk teeth"), which number 20 in
all by age 2. Starting about age 5 or 6, these are
gradually replaced by a permanent set that will total
32 by age 18—when the "wisdom" teeth erupt
through the
gums. The
crown of each
tooth is covered
by shiny white
enamel, the
hardest material
in your body.

*"Baby tooth," about
to be replaced by a
permanent tooth*

Enamel

Dentin

Gum

Jaw bone

The Human Antennae

Sight. Visual information is first received in the form of light rays, which the lens of your eyes focuses as upside-down, reverse images on the retina. Receptor cells, called rods and cones, in the retina change these "light pictures" into electrical signals and feed the information to your brain, which "sees" them in their original form.

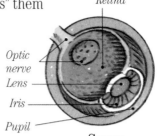

Retina

Optic nerve

Lens

Iris

Pupil

SIGHT

Hearing. Traveling into the wide funnel of your outer ear, sound waves reach your brain through a series of vibrations that begin in the eardrum. This thin piece of skin causes the hammer bone to vibrate and hit the anvil, which activates the stirrup to set up vibrations in the fluid of your inner ear. Nerve endings located here send electrical impulses to your brain, which interprets them so that you can recognize your mother's voice, for example, or tell the difference between the bark of a dog and the song of a bird.

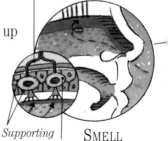

Nerves to brain

Supporting cells

SMELL

Olfactory cells

Smell. Odor molecules—from fresh-baked cookies, let's say—enter your nose and brush against a hidden organ called the olfactory mucous membrane. Receptor cells in the membrane send information to your brain, which recognizes this particular combination of molecules as the smell of cookies.

Taste. Distinguishing one taste from another requires a cooperative effort between your

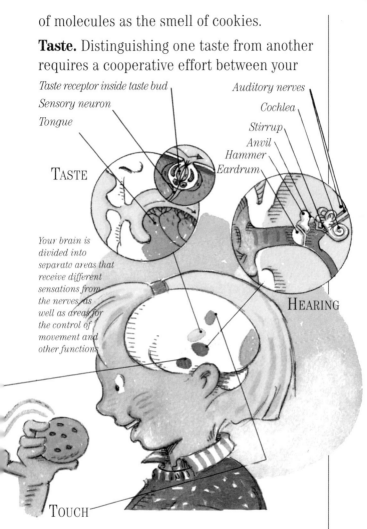

Taste receptor inside taste bud
Sensory neuron
Tongue

Auditory nerves
Cochlea
Stirrup
Anvil
Hammer
Eardrum

TASTE

Your brain is divided into separate areas that receive different sensations from the nerves, as well as areas for the control of movement and other functions

HEARING

TOUCH

tongue and your nose. Taste buds on your tongue tell you whether food is sweet, salty, bitter, sour—or just plain awful. Without the odors transmitted by your nose, however, food would have no flavor at all.

Touch. Information received from touch, the only sense not located within the skull, is transmitted by nerves spread over the skin.

The Message Center:

The Miraculous Brain

Working quietly inside the skull, the brain sorts through an infinite stream of messages from the five senses, stores important information in its memory bank, and takes action when necessary by setting the appropriate muscles in motion. Most thinking is done in the cerebrum, the largest and busiest part of the brain. The left half, or hemisphere, of the cerebrum is responsible for speech and intellectual activities; the right half controls

Impulses travel from the axon of one neuron to the dendrites of another in less than 1/10,000 of a second.

Training the Brain

Every time you learn a new activity, electrical impulses blaze a new path from one motor neuron to another and your brain has to memorize this new pattern of connections. Sometimes, especially if the new activity involves many muscles moving simultaneously, you might have to repeat the movements many times until they're clearly recorded on your mental videotape. That's why learning to ride a bicycle usually requires several tries before it becomes "second nature."

creativity and emotions. A communications system connects the two, so that one side always knows what the other is doing.

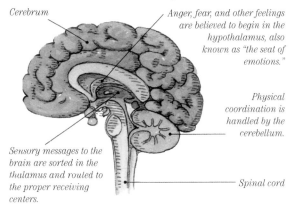

Cerebrum

Anger, fear, and other feelings are believed to begin in the hypothalamus, also known as "the seat of emotions."

Physical coordination is handled by the cerebellum.

Sensory messages to the brain are sorted in the thalamus and routed to the proper receiving centers.

Spinal cord

The Neuron Express

Safeguarded by covering membranes and cushioned by fluid, the brain owes its efficiency to billions of delicate nerve cells called neurons. Each neuron picks up impulses through small fibers called dendrites and passes them on through the axon, a long, single fiber that "connects" with the dendrites of other neurons.

Even though the brain accounts for only 2% of your body weight, 20% of all your energy goes into the billions of connections that occur every second within its nerve tissue. Without these connections, you couldn't think, move, feel—or remember your own name. In fact, you wouldn't be alive!

Each tiny neuron is a transmitter cell that runs on your own chemically fueled electrical system.

The Great Connectors:

The Spine and Spinal Cord

The skull sits on the spine, a snakelike column of 25 separate bones called vertebrae. Also known as the backbone, this column supports your body and protects the spinal cord from injury and disease. Like the links of a bicycle chain, each vertebra allows a little movement so that the spine as a whole enjoys a great deal of flexibility.

The curve of the spine reduces strain on the muscles and allows you to keep your center of gravity over your legs and feet. No matter how loudly someone tells you to "straighten up," you could never straighten your spine all the way.

At the top of the spinal column, the *atlas* vertebra swivels on the *axis* directly beneath

Help, I'm Shrinking!

Believe it or not, you're taller in the morning than at night. Measuring your height against a door frame first thing in the morning, and again in the early evening, will prove that you've lost about a quarter of an inch (half a centimeter) during the day! Gravity and your own daytime activity have compressed the cartilage pads, or disks, between the vertebrae in your spine, causing it to shrink. Don't worry, though: when you're asleep, the cartilage absorbs water from your body and puffs up again.

it, thus allowing you to move your head. The *thoracic* vertebrae each match up with a pair of ribs; the *lumbar* vertebrae carry the weight of your upper body and anchor the heavy muscles of your lower back; and the five fused vertebrae that form the *sacrum* lock the base of the spine to the pelvis.

The final four vertebrae are fused together to form the *coccyx,* or "tailbone." If you had a tail, this is where it would attach!

Brain

Axis
(2nd neck vertebra)

Atlas
(1st neck vertebra)

7 neck vertebrae

Nerves

12 thoracic vertebrae

Your brain weighs only three pounds (1.4 kilograms) but contains 50 to 100 billion nerve cells!

5 lumbar vertebrae

Sacrum

Coccyx

The giraffe's neck, the longest in the animal kingdom, has only seven vertebrae —just like yours.

Some snakes have more than 400 vertebrae, each with matching pair of ribs.

Two-Way Communications

Running through the canal formed by the vertebrae, the spinal cord links your brain with the rest of your body. About three-quarters of an inch (two centimeters) thick, this "nerve trunk" begins with the brain stem, which controls the involuntary muscles used in unconscious actions such as breathing and digestion, and extends all the way down to the first lumbar vertebra. Branching out from the cord are 31 pairs of nerves, each dividing into smaller nerves so that every part of your body can communicate with your brain.

The vast network of nerve cells formed by the spinal cord and brain is known as the central nervous system. Through individual neurons in the nerves, *sensory* information is carried from your body to your brain while *motor* commands are relayed from your brain to your muscles. Neurons extending from the lower part of your spinal cord to your toes can grow to four feet (1.2 meters) in length!

Body Watch

Sometimes the nervous system uses shortcuts to speed up reaction time. If you touch a hot stove, for example, nerves in your hand might send an *"Ouch, it's hot!"* message to your spinal cord, which will immediately send back its own signal: *"Then move your hand!"* The microseconds saved by these unconscious "automatic reflexes" can prevent serious injury.

Feel It In Your Bones

Recruit a friend to help you demonstrate the "kick reflex." Cross one leg over the other at the knee—and relax. Have your friend tap the gap between your kneecap and shinbone with a toy hammer or with stiffened fingers. What happens? Each time your friend taps, the tendons connecting your kneecap to your upper leg bones and muscles jerk your lower leg forward as your thigh and calf muscles contract. This kick reflex is "ordered" by nerve connections from your spinal cord.

Brain

Spinal cord

Cauda equina ("horsetail")

The spinal cord relays information to and from your brain and controls automatic functions such as breathing.

Sciatic nerve

Nerves

Every once in a while, you'll feel a mysterious muscle contraction in your eyelid or cheek. These sudden contractions, or tics, can be caused by "misfires" of nerve signals when you're very tired or under stress.

All Systems Go!

Picture someone tossing you a ball high in the air. Your brain, acting on information from your eyes, follows the ball, estimates its size, and calculates its speed and height as it begins to drop. Simultaneously, messages from your brain to your muscles let you reach toward the ball, stretch, and finally close your hands around it at exactly the right instant. It's only a simple game of catch, but imagine how many computers it would take to control and direct a robot to do that—and to smile after the ball is caught.

The incredible organic computer inside your skull can send electrical signals along some of your body's longer nerves at 300 miles (480 kilometers) per hour. No wonder your reaction time is so fast!

"In With the Good, Out With the Bad":

The Rib Cage and Respiration

S trong, lightweight, and flexible, the rib cage backs up the chest muscles as protection for the lungs, heart, liver, and stomach, as well as some of the major blood vessels.

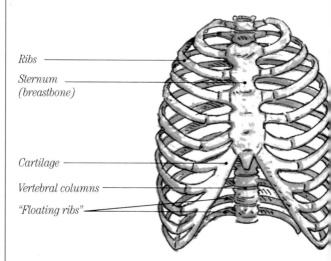

Ribs

Sternum
(breastbone)

Cartilage

Vertebral columns

"Floating ribs"

Feel It In Your Bones

L ean back in a chair, take a deep breath, and feel the shape of your rib cage and the point where your ribs attach to the sternum, or breastbone. The top of this bone is the notch at the base of your throat between the two collarbones.

Although all 12 pairs of ribs are attached to the thoracic vertebrae, only the first seven connect with the sternum, or breastbone. The next three pairs attach to cartilage at the ends of the other ribs. The last two pairs, called "floating" ribs, are held in place only by muscle tissue and do not attach in front.

The ribs can move slightly at the point where they attach to vertebrae and to cartilage in front of the rib cage. Ligaments and muscles between the ribs lift and separate them to allow the lungs to expand. Every time you breathe, your ribs have to move!

Every cell in your body needs oxygen, and it's up to your lungs to keep it in constant supply.

Trachea

Bronchioles (small airways)

Alveoli

Lung

Diaphragm

The Lungs . . .

The respiratory system is responsible for bringing oxygen into your body and releasing waste in the form of carbon dioxide gas. As you breathe in and out, air travels to and from the lungs through a long tube called the trachea. Suspended like long oval sponges within the rib cage, the two lungs are made of special stretchy, but very delicate, tissue that allows them to expand and contract quickly. Inside are clusters of little balloonlike sacs called alveoli, which receive the air through small tubes in the lungs. Believe it or not, several hundred million of these tiny air sacs fill up and empty 15,000 times a day! Oxygen from the air passes through the thin alveolar walls into capillaries, where red blood cells pick it up and carry it to the heart for distribution to the rest of your body.

In exchange for the oxygen, the alveoli receive carbon dioxide from the capillaries. Carbon dioxide, which is waste from the breakdown and use of food by your body, is eliminated when you exhale.

. . . and How You Breathe

The work of the lungs relies on the chest muscles and on the diaphragm, a thick sheet of muscle stretching across the bottom of the chest cavity. As the chest muscles lift the ribs, the diaphragm contracts and pulls downward, giving the lungs more room. The lungs expand in the wider space, and new (or "good") air rushes in to fill the slight vacuum created by the drop in air pressure.

Body Watch

The hairs in your nose are there to catch dust and other undesirable particles that might otherwise find their way to your throat and lungs. Smaller particles that sneak past this first line of defense are swept in a sticky mucus to your nose and mouth, where you can expel them by coughing, blowing your nose, or sneezing. *Atchoo!* Away go the irritating particles, sometimes at hurricane force—over 100 miles (160 kilometers) an hour!

Full of Hot Air!

To see how much air your lungs can hold, you'll need a large plastic jug, a rubber or plastic tube, a marker—and a friend. Fill the jug with water, then fill the sink halfway. Have your friend place one hand over the top of the jug, turn it upside down, and hold it underwater in the sink. Then insert one end of the tube underwater into the neck of the jug. Take a deep breath, place the other end of the tube in your mouth, and blow out as long as you can. The air exhaled from your lungs will displace the water.

Turn the jug right side up and mark the water level, then fill it up again and switch places with your friend.

Whose lungs hold the most air?

When the muscles relax, the air pressure rises, the lungs deflate, and used ("bad") air is forced out through the nose and mouth.

You can control your own respiration but normally the muscles contract and relax on their own to regulate your air supply. When your breathing rate slows down, the diaphragm will even force a wide yawn to take in more air.

Sometimes the diaphragm contracts unexpectedly, causing a case of hiccups. A sudden rush of air strikes the covering flap of the "voicebox," making the vocal cords move and resulting in a series of *hics* that can last for hours!

Your Own Food Processor:

The Digestive System

The digestive system changes what you eat into fuel for your cells and rids your body of everything it can't use. Since you probably eat about half a ton of food each year, this system works overtime!

Digestion starts in the mouth, where saliva softens food as you chew. Small pieces and liquids then squeeze through the esophagus into the stomach, a baglike organ shaped like the letter "J." Here, juices and enzymes break them down into even smaller bits while muscles in the stomach walls churn them into a soupy mixture called chyme. It may take you 20 minutes to eat dinner, but your stomach needs at least three hours to process the food.

Taste Test

Can you taste your food if your sense of smell is temporarily out of commission? Ask an adult to peel and slice a raw potato and an apple. Then cover your eyes and hold your nose as you place them on your tongue and try to tell one from the other. This is one "test" you can't help but fail!

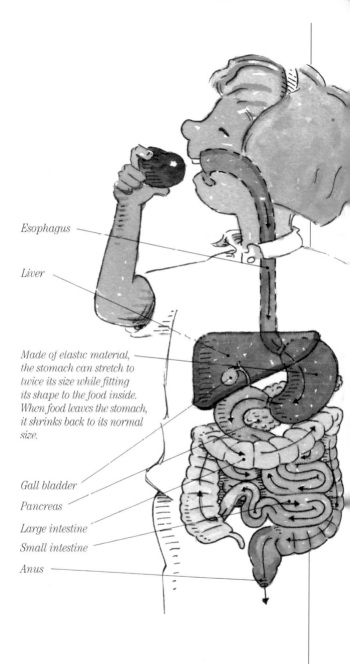

Esophagus

Liver

Made of elastic material, the stomach can stretch to twice its size while fitting its shape to the food inside. When food leaves the stomach, it shrinks back to its normal size.

Gall bladder

Pancreas

Large intestine

Small intestine

Anus

The digestive tube, also known as the alimentary canal, starts in the mouth and ends at the anus—reaching a length of 30 feet (9 meters) in the adult body.

Muscle contractions force the chyme into the small intestine, where capillaries pick up the nutrients for distribution throughout the body. (The small intestine is only "small" in diameter; stretched out, it would reach about 21 feet, or 6.5 meters!) Next, the large intestine (only 5 feet, or 1.5 meters, long) takes the "leftovers," removes the fluid, and passes the waste out through the anus at the end of the line.

Digestive Aids

Also at work in the digestive process are two organs that leak their contents into the small intestine. The liver, curved up under the diaphragm, pours acid bile into the intestine; the pancreas, behind the stomach, secretes additional enzymes. The liver is especially helpful in breaking down fat into nutrients that the body can easily use.

The two bean-shaped kidneys, found below the rib cage and behind the intestines on either side of the spinal column, contribute to digestion by regulating fluids and salt in the body and ridding the blood of wastes,

The All-Purpose Tongue

Many sets of muscles, running in different directions, give your tongue an extraordinary amount of versatility. You use it for tasting food, for making separate sounds when you speak, and also for swallowing. The base of your tongue, far down your throat, is attached to the hyoid bone—a U-shaped bone that is loosely connected to the base of your skull and forms a link to your trachea and esophagus.

which pass to the bladder in the form of urine. Working surprisingly hard for their size, the kidneys filter 425 gallons (1,600 liters) of blood each day!

Body Watch

Directly in front of the esophagus is the trachea, or breathing tube. When you're ready to swallow a mouthful of food, the trachea knows to close the epiglottis—a little "trap door" behind the tongue. If a mix-up occurs, and food enters the trachea by mistake, choking is the uncomfortable consequence.

Swallowed food passes into a 10-inch pipe called the esophagus. The pipe's muscles squeeze each mouthful of food and push it through a "door" that opens to let it pass into the stomach.

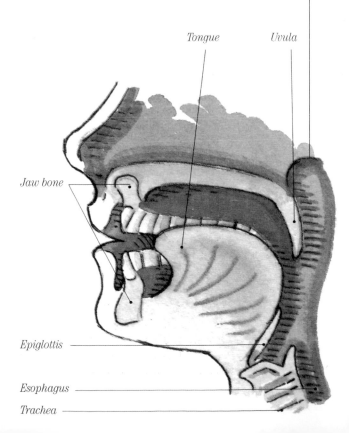

Tongue

Uvula

Jaw bone

Epiglottis

Esophagus

Trachea

A Good Look at Your Limbs:

The Arms and Legs

The arms and legs are the most visible parts of the body, yet it's hard not to take them for granted. After all, they seem to move by themselves, providing balance and support as if they had minds of their own.

You probably never noticed the many similarities between your arms and legs, an inheritance from the early human ancestors who walked on all fours. Both sets of limbs begin at the top with one large bone, attached to the body with the same kind of joint (pages 48–50). And each lower limb has two separate bones, connected to the upper limb by a similar joint.

Feel It In Your Bones

It's easy to touch the ends of your lower arm and leg bones. You can feel the top of the ulna as the large, jutting point of your elbow and its bottom end as a knob at the outside of your wrist. At the base of your thumb, on the near side of the wrist, is the bottom of the radius. Similarly, at the outside of your ankle, you can feel the knobby end of the fibula (what we call the ankle bone); at the inside of the ankle is the end of the tibia.

Unlike the bones whose main job is to protect your organs, the arm and leg bones are used chiefly for leverage and locomotion. These bones allow the arms to swing from the shoulders, while the legs swing from the hips.

Has your leg or foot ever "fallen asleep"? This happens after you've been sitting with your legs crossed, with one leg pressing on a nerve (and sometimes a blood vessel) in the other leg and preventing its signals from getting to your brain. When you change position and release the pressure, the nerve signals suddenly flood your brain and you feel a sensation known as "pins and needles."

Of course, there are obvious differences, too, in their size and the jobs they do. Your arms are smaller than your legs, with weaker muscles, because they don't have to support your whole body and move you along. On the other hand, fewer muscles are needed in your legs because less flexibility is required of them.

Also, unlike the lower leg bones, the radius and ulna in the lower arm are nearly the same size and can swivel with each other when you want to turn the palm of your hand up or down. In the leg, the large tibia, or shinbone, contributes more support than the thin fibula and is very sensitive to bumps because of its nearness to the skin.

The kneecap has no counterpart in the arm. What we call the "funny bone" in the elbow is actually a nerve running over the end of the ulna behind the humerus. A bump on this nerve can send a tingling shock all the way down to your fingers!

Nature's Knee Guard

About the same size as the "pocket" of your palm, the kneecap bone, or patella, is not connected directly to the other leg bones but instead is embedded in a large tendon in front of the knee. From this vantage point, it can shield the important knee joint and anchor some of the powerful leg muscles.

Femur

Patella

Tibia

Fibula

The Amazing Opposable Thumb

The single most important feature of the human hand is the unique "saddle joint" that lets you move your thumb from a stretched-out position all the way across your palm and "oppose" or touch each fingertip along the way. In combination with your brain, this makes your hand a really incredible tool, capable of making beautiful art, fixing a bicycle, or snapping your fingers.

Lacking this type of joint, your big toe is not equipped for gripping things (although it can probably pick a marble off the floor). You use its strength to push off the ground every time you take a step and you rely on it for balance whenever you stand on "tiptoe."

On Hands and Feet

The 8 bones of the wrist, and the 19 bones of the hand and fingers, work with the muscles in an ingenious system of levers and pincers.

The foot and ankle together have 26 bones, 33 joints, and more than 100 ligaments, which together support your body, keep you moving, and prevent you from falling over. Designed for weight-bearing and movement, rather than for delicate actions, the foot has less flexible joints than the hand and its digits are shorter. The slight arch on the inside of the foot, with its ability to flatten out, acts as a natural, built-in shock absorber.

Where Two Bones Meet:
Joint Efforts

The joints of the skeleton are the sites where two bones articulate, or come together. (Even the tiny ear bones have their own miniature joints!) *Stationary* joints, such as those between the vertebrae and between the bones of the skull, allow little or no movement. *Movable* joints, which enable the skeleton to bend and twist, are oiled by synovial fluid and held together by bands of tough, fibrous tissue called ligaments. So that two bones move easily against each other, the weight-bearing surfaces are covered by smooth cartilage.

Feel It In Your Bones

To see how much "play" a ball-and-socket joint allows, push your shoulders and elbows back as far as they'll go. Now bring your shoulders and arms forward to a rounded position. These movements involve the triangle-shaped scapula (shoulder bone) on each side, the clavicle (collarbone), and the humerus, which fits into the shoulder socket. Because each scapula is attached at the back only by muscle, the clavicle's job is to tie the scapula to the sternum (breastbone) and strengthen the shoulder joint.

In addition to the saddle joint at the base of the thumb, which allows movement up and down and from side to side, there are three major kinds of joints with varying degrees of mobility. Ball-and-socket joints, where the arms and legs connect with the body at the shoulders and hips, permit movement in almost every direction. Hinge joints, which connect the separate arm and leg bones at the

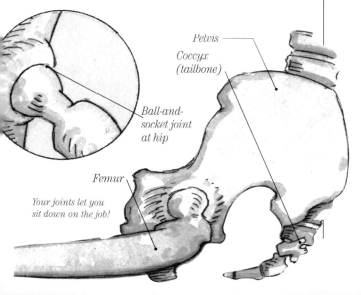

Pelvis

Coccyx
(tailbone)

Ball-and-socket joint
at hip

Femur

*Your joints let you
sit down on the job!*

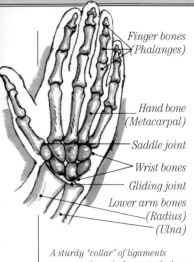

Finger bones
(Phalanges)

Hand bone
(Metacarpal)

Saddle joint

Wrist bones

Gliding joint

Lower arm bones
(Radius)
(Ulna)

*A sturdy "collar" of ligaments
connects the wrist bones to the bones
of the lower arm. The individual
wrist bones move against each other.*

People who can
do "splits," or
almost touch their
thumb to the inside
of their arm, aren't
actually double-
jointed—there's
no such thing as
having two joints
at the same
location. Their
unusual dexterity
springs from very
flexible ligaments
that give their
joints a wider than
average range of
movement.

elbow and knee, work like the hinges of a door
and restrict movement to one direction only.

The third major kind of joint connects the
hand to the arm at the wrist, and the foot to
the leg at the ankle. This gliding, or "swivel,"
joint allows the wrist and ankle bones to
overlap and slide from side to side at the ends
of the arm and leg bones, enabling the wrists
and ankles to bend and rotate.

Teamwork

Joints not only permit movement, but also
"give" to absorb shocks to the body. When you
jump down from a fence, for example, your
feet flex, or bend at the toes, as you hit the
ground. Your body weight then transfers back
toward your heels as your arches flex—along
with your ankles, knees, and hip joints.
Meanwhile, joints in your arms, head, and
back also help you adjust your balance.

The Largest Organ of All:
The Skin

Your entire body is wrapped up in skin, a mostly smooth, somewhat hairy, waterproof sack that accounts for 12% of your weight.

The skin has several important jobs. In addition to making you look good, it holds in your body fluids, helps regulate your temperature, cushions and protects you, and helps defend against disease. It even forms ridges and grooves to allow your fingers and toes to get a good grip.

In the outer layer of skin, called the *epidermis,* special cells manufacture a pigment called melanin. Variations in skin color, including freckles, are caused by this pigment, as are different shades of hair color. Melanin is useful because it protects the skin from sunburn. When you spend a lot of time in the sun, granules of melanin are released and you get a tan.

The thick bottom layer of skin, the *dermis,* contains blood vessels, elastic fibers, and fat.

Uninvited Guests

Tiny living organisms called bacteria cover your body from head to toe. Baths and showers wash some down the drain, and perspiration carries others away, but at this very moment nearly 20 *million* "visitors" occupy every square inch on some parts of your body surface! Don't worry, though—most of them are either harmless or helpful.

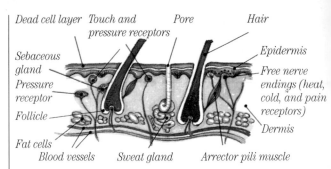

Dead cell layer | Touch and pressure receptors | Pore | Hair
Sebaceous gland | Epidermis
Pressure receptor | Free nerve endings (heat, cold, and pain receptors)
Follicle
Dermis
Fat cells
Blood vessels | Sweat gland | Arrector pili muscle

Nerve endings in the dermis send temperature, pain, touch, and other sensory information to the brain.

Every hour, the skin has to make about one and a half million new cells just to replace all the cells that wear out in this short time span. In fact, the dead skin cells shed by the body are a major part of the dust in many homes!

Hair-Raisers

Did you know that hair is made mostly of dead skin cells? Only the base of each hair is alive.

Rooted in the dermis, hair grows up through the epidermis and out the pores. The skin of your scalp probably contains the roots of more

Body Watch

Strange as it seems, perspiring, or sweating, cools you off. When nerves in the skin tell the brain that your body is heating up, the brain signals the sweat glands to go to work. There are about 650 sweat glands in each square inch of skin—more than two million in all. The salty sweat they produce squirts out to the skin surface through tiny openings called *pores*. As the sweat evaporates, your skin cools off and your body temperature drops.

Hard as Nails

The main ingredient in your hair is keratin, a tough, fibery protein that also waterproofs and protects your skin. *Claws and hooves are made of keratin, too, and so are horns, but not antlers!* Calluses form on the palms of your hands and the soles of your feet when keratin accumulates to protect these areas from prolonged rubbing and pressure. This same stiffening protein is found in your nails, which are actually nothing more than specialized skin cells growing from the ends of your fingers and toes!

than 100,000 hairs. The world's record for long hair is 25 feet— that's a lot of dead cells!

On a cold day, you can see how your skin and hair react to temperature. As little muscles contract around the hair follicles, the hairs straighten up. (In furry animals, this traps a layer of warm air next to the skin, but people don't have that much hair.) The muscle contraction also causes the skin to bulge up, forming "goose bumps." Your body sometimes has the same reaction when you're really scared.

The process of aging can be noticed clearly in the skin and hair. Over the years, the skin thins out, becomes drier, and loses elasticity in the sun. What's more, the melanin supply begins to dwindle, turning your hair gray or white as its natural color "fades."

Shivering is another way your body responds to cold temperatures. Very rapid muscle contractions help warm you up!

Inside the Pelvis

The pelvis, or hip bone, appears to be a single, bowl-shaped bone, but in fact it comprises six bones in all. These bones cradle the spine and important organs in the lower torso.

On each side of your body, you can feel the top, curved edge of the ilium, the largest of these bones, flaring out just below your waist. Beneath the ilium, at the front end of the pelvis, is the pubis. And at the lower back is the ischium, which forms a loop with the pubis and comes closest to touching the seat of a chair when you sit down.

The Gender Gap

Along with the bladder and intestines, most of the organs that account for the differences

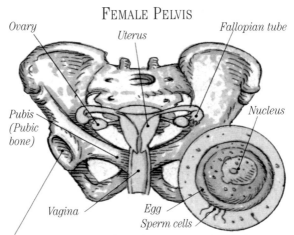

FEMALE PELVIS

Ovary *Uterus* *Fallopian tube*

Pubis (Pubic bone)

Nucleus

Vagina *Egg* *Sperm cells*

The three pelvic bones from each side of your body fuse together to form the acetabulum, the cup-shaped socket where the round head of the thighbone fits. The bones of your pelvis won't completely fuse at this hip joint until you're a teenager.

MALE PELVIS

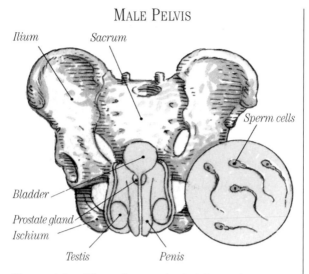

Ilium
Sacrum
Sperm cells
Bladder
Prostate gland
Ischium
Testis
Penis

The most obvious difference between a female skeleton and a male skeleton is in the shape of the pelvis. This helps scientists determine whether human fossil skeletons originally belonged to men or women.

between men and women are found inside the bowl of the pelvis.

In the female pelvis are the egg-producing ovaries and the uterus, where you began life as a fertilized egg. The male pelvis encloses the prostate gland, involved in producing and delivering the sperm that fertilize the egg.

The female pelvis is usually wider, shallower, and less robust than the male pelvis, with more room between the pubic bones and sacrum. In addition, the female sacrum is shorter, wider, and less curved, while the coccyx just beneath it is capable of more movement.

These gender differences in the arrangement of pelvic bones reflect the woman's child-bearing role. Her pelvis must be roomy and expandable to make childbirth possible.

Special Delivery

The female pelvis actually participates in childbirth! When a baby is ready to be delivered, after nine months inside the uterus, the mother's pubic bones push slightly apart at the pubic joint to widen the birth canal.

The shape of the mother's pelvis also affects the baby's position during its journey. Because the bones leave more space crosswise than from top to bottom, and the baby's head is widest from back to front, the baby turns sideways on its way through the canal to meet the outside world.

Human beings experience three big growth spurts: 1) before birth, when the fetus inside the mother increases its weight about 2.4 billion times; 2) between birth and the age of two; 3) at puberty, when young teenagers can grow 4 to 6 inches (10 to 15 centimeters) in a single year!

Fractures, Pulls, Twists, and Sprains

For all its toughness and strength, the human skeleton is vulnerable to occasional fractures—or broken bones. Hit hard enough, or forced in the wrong direction, a bone can crack, splinter, or even snap in two. But thanks to its living cells, the same bone can "knit" itself back together again under a doctor's supervision.

X-ray pictures tell the doctor the exact nature of a bone break. Showing the skin and internal organs as light, misty shadows, these pictures highlight the bones and joints to reveal even "hairline" fractures.

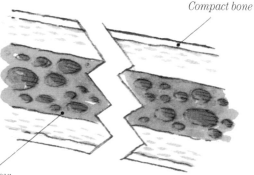

Compact bone

Marrow

A simple fracture like this can be easily set by a doctor. A compound fracture, when the broken bone sticks out through the skin, is much more serious.

In the first stage of bone repair, osteoblasts bridge the fracture with fibers of collagen, which is then cemented together with mineral crystals to form new bone and a strong bond.

If the break is serious enough, the doctor will set the separate parts of bone in their proper position before applying a splint or protective cast to keep the bone from moving. Sometimes stainless-steel plates and screws are needed to hold the pieces together while the bone mends.

Bone repair is similar to the growth process. First, fibers of protein material bridge the gap between the pieces of bone to create a temporary bond. Next, the bone-making osteoblasts move into the area, grow larger, and harden the fibers into true bone. And finally, since the site of the break can be a little lumpy with extra bone growth, special bone-destroying cells called osteoclasts dissolve away the rough edges and make the finished mend smooth.

Once mended, the break will be almost invisible. And the bone will probably be as strong as ever!

Muscle and Joint Injuries

In sports and other strenuous activities,

injuries can occur in muscles or in the tendons that attach them to bones. Minor tears in muscle fibers happen all the time and mend themselves when the body is at rest. Muscle pulls, or stretched tendons, heal with therapy and rest. If a tendon actually pulls away from the bone, however, surgery is required to repair the injury.

Most injuries to joints occur when sudden force bends a ligament farther than it can stretch or twists it in the wrong direction. Many athletes sustain knee injuries when their weight shifts unexpectedly in a direction that the knee can't follow, wrenching the ligaments that hold the femur and tibia together. The same thing happens when you step into a hole, or off the sidewalk the wrong way, and you sprain your ankle. Applying ice and resting the injured joint is usually sufficient, although severe ligament tears may call for surgical tape and sometimes even a cast to limit movement during the healing process.

In the second stage of repair, osteoclasts move in to smooth over or destroy any rough patches of extra bone built up by the osteoblasts.

The Way We Were . . .

Human beings today are all one species—one kind of animal—in the same way that all horses are one species. Humans, like racehorses, circus ponies, and giant draft horses, have a lot of variety in physical appearance. Professional basketball players and African pygmies, straight-haired blondes and curly redheads, and people with black, brown, yellow, red, or white skin all share enough of the same genes to be one species. Our species has the scientific name *Homo sapiens,* which means "wise man."

You may be better at baseball or operating a computer, but out in the woods your distant ancestor could do a better job of hunting and gathering food for dinner.

A fossil nicknamed Lucy, found in Ethiopia, told us a lot about what we once looked like. From the skeletal bones, dating back 3.5 million years, scientists concluded that Lucy was probably a human ancestor. The shape of the pelvis showed that the bones were those of a woman and that she walked nearly upright. Footprints of the same age have also been found in Africa, made in mud and ash and now hardened into stone.

The earliest humanlike ancestors were not *Homo sapiens.* They were different enough to belong to different species. If you had a time machine, or could look at lots of fossil skeletons, you would see that the human body has gone through many changes over the years. Fossil remains of the earliest humans and their ancestors tell us that our frames are more slender and less muscular than theirs, and that we stand taller and straighter than they did. Early humans were generally more rugged-looking, with bony ridges over their eyes, and jaws that jutted forward to hold their large teeth. They probably had a lot more body hair.

The pelvis was one of the major changes in the human skeleton. Unlike the pelvis of an animal which walks on all fours, ours has assumed a

What's In Your Genes

Genes, found inside your body's cells, are molecules of hereditary material that you get from each of your parents. Your unique combination of DNA (deoxyribonucleic acid)—the stuff of which genes are made—determines what you look like and how your body functions.

A tiny species of hobbitlike human, *Homo floresiensis,* lived in Indonesia as recently as 18,000 years ago. Adults of this species stood only about 3 feet high!

rounded, upright shape that lines up the legs with the spine and enables us to stand erect. This posture allows the legs to carry our weight and frees the hands for other work.

The shape of the cranium has also changed to accommodate a larger brain. Early human skulls were lower in the forehead and longer at the back, indicating that the front of the brain—where intelligence, thought, memory, and sensory interpretations are centered— was less developed than ours. Physical coordination and automatic responses, controlled by the cerebellum at the back of the skull, were far more important millions of years ago.

Where Do We Go From Here?

In the past, human species and the way they look have changed, sometimes as the result of big changes in the environment. During the Ice Age, glaciers covered much of North America and Europe. People who could not adapt to the cold did not live long enough to have children. Some did adapt, and lived to reproduce because they had small differences that allowed them to survive the cold and the hard life. These people passed on those physical differences to their children. Probably the best at surviving the cold were the Neanderthals. They had big noses which helped warm the air before it went into their lungs, deep chests, and big muscles, which helped them hunt bison and mammoths. They probably also had lots of body hair. As the world's climate warmed, these characteristics were no longer necessary to survive. Our species moved into the area, equipped with a brain that was better at technology and organization. We were able to use resources more effectively, and the Neanderthals soon became extinct.

Sometimes things that look like disadvantages don't turn out to be a problem. For millions of years, our ancestors had big jaws and very large, sometimes huge, teeth. Big teeth and jaws were necessary to chew tough foods, and people born with smaller teeth didn't do so well. Small teeth wore out quickly from bits of shell, grit, and hard, raw plant material, and, without teeth, people starved to death early in life. After people learned how to grow food, and once food began to be washed and cooked, having small teeth wasn't a problem. Small-toothed people began living long enough to have children, who in turn inherited the gene for small teeth. Now people all over the world have small teeth. Small teeth aren't better; having them just stopped being a disadvantage. Advances in medicine and technology are doing a lot to balance out many things that used to be disadvantages for our species.

What about other trends in human evolution? Do people really need to have tonsils and an appendix? People get along fine without them, and without wisdom teeth too. Will humans in the future have these "extra" body parts, or will they disappear? The best answer for that question is to ask one or two more: Will a person born without an appendix, tonsils, or wisdom teeth have any advantage over people born with them? Is he or she more likely to survive and reproduce successfully? The answer to both is probably no. Humans may be stuck with those extra bits!

Many people are convinced that changes to the environment will be as destructive to our species as it was to the Neanderthals. With increased air and water pollution and damage to the ozone layer, perhaps people with tougher skin that's resistant to ultra-violet radiation and those with less chemical sensitivity will be better survivors. Or maybe once again, improved medicine and better technology will come to the rescue.

Will our brains and skulls get larger? Will we have as many toes? Your thoughts and predictions are just as valuable as those of the scientists and science-fiction writers who think about these matters. One thing is certain. All life forms change, however slowly, and, someday, the human skeleton will have a new look!